2/13/1958 +

# ROUAULT

# *Rouault*

*Text and Notes by*
JOSHUA KIND
Illinois Institute of Technology

TUDOR PUBLISHING COMPANY
*New York*

# ROUAULT: MELANCHOLY EXPRESSIONIST

Rouault's art is most easily understood when one sees his work as a part of that 20th-century vision labelled "Expressionism." This is an art which conveys emotions and thoughts directly, without a careful description of visual reality. Distortion is practiced with the aim of conveying the artist's inner feelings.

In Rouault's paintings the expressionist devices—fierce color, heavy outlines, simplified drawing, crude texture—all work to produce an effect varying from moral anguish to a lyrical despair. It must be said that this artistic non-allegiance to the factual world can be found throughout the history of art and especially so among religious artists such as El Greco or Rembrandt. Still, the crudeness and brutality of Rouault's use of these devices move many people to reject his work at first, along with that of other artists who renounced traditional means.

In Pl. 1, a painting made in 1894, when Rouault was still a student, one can easily recognize the traditional qualities: the careful drawing with fluid outlines, the realistic description of the volumes of the figures. A comparison of this work, so transparently academic in style, with the paintings of 1903 (Pls. 4 and 5) reveals the length of the step Rouault took in the decade 1895–1905, in the Europewide reaction of young artists of the time against the rigid and unfeeling procedures of their elders. And his works of the next decade depart still further, paralleling not the Parisian scene, but rather developments in Germany, particularly among such artists as Nolde and Kirchner.

If there is any important distinction between Rouault and other far-seeing artists of his age, it is that Rouault is uniquely a religious artist—even in those works that do not present a Christian subject. And by some, Rouault is considered the most important 20th-century religious artist.

## EARLY YEARS

Georges Rouault was born on the 27th of May, 1871, and the circumstances of his birth provide the biographer with a proper kind of portent of the dark and troubled paintings of the future. The section of the city of Paris, Belleville, where his parents lived, was under bombardment on that day by the troops of the government, and so his mother, Marie-Louise, was carried to the cellar to give birth to Georges. His father, Alexandre, was a quiet man, a cabinet maker employed at the Pleyel piano factory as a wood-finisher.

The generally impoverished existence of the boy was often relieved by visits to the home of his maternal grandfather; this man, a minor railway worker, although as poor as his son-in-law, had a feeling for art. Rouault would later recall the walks he would take with his grandfather along the banks of the Seine, searching in the book stalls for reproductions of Manet, Daumier and Courbet. And it is touching to note that Rouault's first exhibited work, in the 1890's, would bear the name Georges Rouault-Champdavoine, his mother's name appended, perhaps in tribute to his grandfather who had died ten years before.

At the age of 14, in 1885, Rouault was forced to abandon school—he had just passed his high-school entrance exams—and take a job. Looking back upon his life and work, many critical surveys of Rouault's achievement insist on the importance for his artistic outlook of these years spent both as a stained-glass maker and (more vitally) repairer. The distinction is important, because the style in which glass was made in the later 19th century was analogous to that style which we have just called "traditional." This academic style, that is, style of the schools, tried always for a perfected beauty, drew on the sheets of glass as if they were paper, and used very thin pieces of lead to hold the sheets together. The desired effect was that of a painting of the time. In contrast, the older glass of the 12th, 13th and 14th centuries that came in for repair could be called "cruder," but only if one holds that the svelte style of the High Renaissance, and therefore the academic art of the 19th century, was the ultimate standard of excellence. This old glass had thicker pieces of lead and large areas of brilliant color with little representational or imitational intention—the source, then, some say, of the effects seen in the pictures which Rouault began to make about the year 1903 (cf. Pl. 4) and which became quite pronounced in the later paintings (cf. Pl. 34).

Rouault's formative years were also strongly affected by his family's social Catholicism. His father had sent Rouault to a Protestant school as a protest against the Papal condemnation of the Catholic social democrat Lemennais, whose writings the elder Rouault fervently admired. Under the succeeding Pope

Leo XIII, there was a powerful attempt made to reconcile the innate conservatism of Catholic church doctrine with both science and society; in France, this movement for a more socially responsible Catholicism, called the *ralliement*, was especially important, since there was not only a long Gallic tradition of intellectual anti-clericalism, but also an entrenched and aggressive philosophy of Positivism. It should be noted, though, that Rouault's life and work are generally apart from any programmatic social protest, even though one of his early works, *The Work Yard* (1897, Pl. 2), is filled with the uneasiness of revolution. In his mature work, from the 1903 period on, the protest and the despair of his clowns, judges and prostitutes will be his own, an individual cry for justice and love. This will in no way lessen the power of his art; in fact, unlinked as it was to dogma, either religious or secular, his message had the possibility of being more widely understood.

## MOREAU

The next great influence in the young man's life was to be the mysterious painter Gustave Moreau, who taught at the École Nationale des Beaux-Arts, which Rouault attended after having decided to become a painter. Moreau, although firmly committed to a Romantic, exotic, perhaps even neurotic artistic style, was nonetheless a great teacher. His own painting was characterized by a minute technique, a fantastic aura, faint color, yet carefully rendered details composed in great contrasts of lights and darks. Although he made no attempt to force this style upon his students, Rouault's *Child Jesus Among the Doctors* (Pl. 1) shows the influence of Moreau in the way the story is told (tiny figures in the huge, gloomy temple, carefully drawn as a retelling of a literary narrative) as well as Rouault's innate predilection for a freer, broader style—in this case learned no doubt from his acquaintance with the work of Rembrandt at the Louvre.

Yet Moreau had another side to his art; and no one knew this better than Rouault. For Moreau at the time of his death in 1898 directed the French government to take over his entire house and collection of his own work, and to preserve the latter intact so that the sense of his effort as an artist would survive. After some years of organizational and legal difficulties, the Gustave Moreau Museum opened in 1903, with Rouault appointed curator, a post he was to hold to the end of his life. Of course, even before this, Rouault was aware of the scope of his master's work, for as a student he had had access to the mysterious house where Moreau carefully stored his hundreds of works. But the appointment was to insure (it was not really necessary) that Rouault would be kept within the hold of this fascinating personality whose attitudes and artistic techniques permeate the whole of Rouault's evolution.

In his private work Moreau was a symbolist. Put most simply, what he wished to do was to suggest rather than describe, to create a mood, vague and half-formed, rather than retell a literary story. It is ironic but understandable that he is so often accused of being a precise and fastidious literary painter—the public knew only the large "salon" paintings, where this charge is quite true. Nevertheless these carefully finished works were only half of his endeavor. The other half—his watercolors and small oils—were wild, chaotic, richly hued, and often contained almost unrecognizable forms and great sheets of color. They must be seen to understand fully both their influence on Rouault and the meaning of Symbolism. Although Rouault was soon to abandon the story-telling pictures of the public Moreau, the effect of Moreau's Symbolist works was to make itself felt long afterwards.

## THE GOSPEL OF SUFFERING

In the years following the death of Moreau, Rouault, by no means a young student any longer, searched for some guiding force. Influenced by his understanding of the Post-impressionists—such artists as Van Gogh, Cézanne and Degas—he abandoned the literary picture and tried his hand at the "new" art, which portrayed the actualities of urban and rural life. Pl. 3 is a work from this time when he painted in the open air as a method of achieving a fresh vigor, just as the Impressionists had done some 40 years before. Yet for Rouault this was not the right path.

In the face of a growing anti-Catholic reaction in France, and overcome with fatigue at the violence of life in Paris, he sought refuge in the Catholic colony at Liguge in April of 1901. He was to remain there for five months, until the dissolution of the retreat under a new law prohibiting religious communities. During these few months Rouault, who had recently begun some literary attempts of his own, was greatly moved by his acquaintance with one of the most influential figures of French literature, the legendary Joris-Carl Huysmans (1848–1907). Huysmans had worked his way through a literary career which included a novel considered the first to treat the theme of prostitution, to a nihilistic climax in *À Rebours* (*Against the Grain*), a work dealing with decadent aestheticism—the search for pleasure in a world where the usual sources no longer sufficed. At that point, Huysmans had become a Catholic convert, finally renouncing the world which had so deeply troubled him. But while Rouault was stirred by Huysman's philosophy, his art was not affected by the Symbolist finesse of Huysman's later work; the artist was seeking a more compelling father figure and would soon find him.

During these decisive first years of the century when his style was maturing, Rouault became friendly with the incredible and violent Catholic writer Leon Bloy. Twenty-five years older than Rouault, Bloy was the inventor of the modern Catholic novel, with two books that deeply affected Rouault: *Le Désespéré* (1887) and *La Pauvre* (1897). Both deal with themes of suffering, redemption and the rejection of the sordidness of this world. Rouault's style at this time may be said to parallel that anguish of Bloy's so well seen in the writer's words: "I have meditated long and often on suffering, I am now convinced that nothing else is supernatural in this world. All the rest is human." The two men remained firm friends until Bloy's death in 1917, despite Bloy's absolute non-comprehension of what it was that Rouault was doing in his new manner—exemplified by the rough, dark, blue works of the first days of their friendship (cf. Pl. 8).

## DEVELOPMENT OF STYLE

Rouault had begun working in this new manner a short time before. Avant-garde Paris in those years was being infiltrated by "primitivism"—a love of color and form for its own sake, a feeling for rough handling and the thrill of direct sensation exuded by simple and direct forms. All this was a specific aspect of the larger phenomenon called Expressionism, and was influenced by the work of Van Gogh and Cézanne and the sculpture of primitive peoples. Rouault reacted to this style, but not at all to its subject matter, which remained traditional—still-lifes, landscapes, figures in interiors.

He had known Matisse since their days at Moreau's studio, and now they came together once more as participants in a new exhibition to which the younger advanced artists contributed—the Autumn Salon. Here, in 1905, the *Fauves* ("wild beasts"), were christened. The group included Matisse as leader, Marquet and Vlaminck, and because three of his works (cf. Pls. 8, 9, 11) were hung in the 1905 show, Rouault was also taken to be a member. Actually, Rouault never closely associated himself with this movement. The Fauves were in love with life, and painted in rich, exuberant hues where the pulsation of the brushstroke was a sign of power and virtuosity; in the work of Rouault these elements were a moral condemnation.

Rouault was a sincere Catholic believer, and while his typical subject matter of this period, the clowns, the prostitutes, the demi-monde, move quite far from his Moreau-influenced work, where at least careful painting and an explicit Christian or biblical story could be found, his paintings are filled (as they will be throughout his life) with a "moral preoccupation." They are religious works rather than works with religious subjects.

Recently, in 1965, the family of Rouault presented to the French State many of the artist's unfinished paintings. When exhibited for the first time (at the Tate Gallery in London) the works of his early years revealed how self-conscious was Rouault's rejection of easeful styles and subjects. He could paint an arabesque like Bonnard, an asymmetrical composition like Vuillard, or achieve a richly exuberant plasticity like Soutine. Yet these exercises in these many styles remained unfinished. He had chosen not to explore them, for his spirit was elsewhere.

## VOLLARD

About 1910, as he began to exhibit often—and became a favorite target of critical vituperation because of the obscenity and vileness of his subject matter and the grating looseness of his handling—Rouault was introduced to the man who would soon control his artistic life. This was Ambroise Vollard, the picture dealer, who had since 1892 achieved some success by selling the works of Cézanne (whose first one-man show he had held in 1895), Bonnard, Gauguin, Picasso, Van Gogh, and many other avant-garde artists. Vollard had then gone on to satisfy his dream of becoming a great book publisher by investing his money in the publication of finely crafted portfolios of prints, and ultimately in books illustrated by the same advanced artists whose paintings and sculpture he had sold (Munch, Redon, Vuillard, Maillol and others). In 1913, Vollard bought up all of the works in Rouault's studio, and in 1917 he became the artist's sole agent, buying whatever the artist produced. The relationship between these two men was a delicate and intimate one: Vollard made a studio for Rouault on the top floor of his own home, and during the next decade Rouault occupied himself a good deal with the creation of steel plates for book illustration. Many of these plates, on which the artist worked as intensively as on his paintings, are counted among the 20th century's greatest graphic art.

## THE MAJOR PHASE

The two decades between the wars saw the full development of the painting style for which Rouault is best known: that rich, glowing oil color thickly encrusted between heavy black contour lines. Several of his greatest paintings are from this period, for instance, *The Three Judges* (1924, Pl. 28) and the *Old King* (1937, Pl. 48). His subject matter changed hardly at all. The themes which he had come upon during the time of his first maturity—the circus, the world of vice, the judge, the oppressed workers in their slums, the Passion story—all these remain, with no real additions to the repertoire. And none are really necessary for an artist of Rouault's temperament, for whom, it has been said, art is a "ritual," a compulsive and cathartic act, like the Catholic Mass. Little varied, it always carries intense and unspeakable satisfaction. In this obsessive performance, Rouault is like the sculptor Alberto Giacometti (1901–1966), if only in the sameness and repetition of his production over the course of many years. It is unquestionable that the process was far more satisfying for Rouault, given not only his religion, but also his non-attachment to any of the 20th-century aesthetic values other than style.

The years following World War I witnessed an increasing recognition of Rouault's unique talents. "The only true religious painter of our time" is a very apt phrase often applied to him. Yet even with the coming of fame, Rouault's life went on very much as before. Each day saw his appearance in Vollard's studio to which almost no one was admitted. Except for an occasional visit to

Switzerland he hardly ever traveled. He had always been intrigued by the Medieval Christian ideal of artistic anonymity—the artist at work in the praise of God and caring little for the course of his work after its production (note his portrait as an apprentice, Pl. 36)—and his contract with Vollard freed him from financial distractions.

## LAST YEARS

Rouault invariably refrained from signing or dating his works until he felt they were completely finished—the signing perhaps only a kind of concession to modern necessity. And so hundreds of paintings, to which Rouault went back as time and inspiration permitted, accumulated over the years in his studio in the household of Vollard. After World War II, the heirs of the art dealer, who died in 1939, claimed that all these works were the legal possession of the Vollard estate, since by contract all work completed by Rouault became the property of Vollard. In a famous lawsuit brought in 1947 by the artist and his friends, their claim, which was upheld by the courts, was that all this work, unsigned and undated, was unfinished, and therefore still in the possession of the artist, the artist alone having the right to say when a work is complete. About one year later, in an equally publicized event, the artist threw into a furnace more than 300 canvases culled from more than 700 given back to him by the Vollard heirs. Rouault said simply that his motive was not profound; he was an old man, over 75, and had not time enough properly to finish these paintings which he found least advanced toward completion.

Later that year, 1948, Rouault did have the satisfaction of seeing one of his life's major projects completed. The great *Miserere* was finally published. In the earliest days of their association, in 1914, Vollard and Rouault had conceived two great volumes comprising 100 plates, the *Miserere* and the *Guerre*. In the 1930's, when 58 plates had been completed, a single volume with these names was announced. Now Vollard was notoriously slow in the final production of his commissioned books—de luxe volumes in limited editions printed on the finest paper. He is fondly remembered by Rouault in the preface to the 1948 edition of the *Miserere*, as it was finally titled: ". . . let us agree that he had taste and a keen desire to make beautiful books without breaking any speed records, but it would have taken three centuries to bring to perfection the various works and paintings with which, in utter disregard of earthly limitations, he wished to burden the pilgrim."

Still, Vollard's last two books published before his death were Rouault's: in 1938, the *Cirque de l'Etoile Filante* (*Circus of the Shooting Star*); and in 1939, Suarès' text of the *Passion*, the paintings for several of the chapters of which are in this book (Pls. 75–78). The complex process of the creation of these illustrated books is discussed in the notes. And previously, in 1932, still another book, *The Reincarnation of Father Ubu*, had been published. Two remain unpublished: Baudelaire's *Flowers of Evil* and Saurès' *The Circus*.

The last ten years of Rouault's life were spent perfecting those paintings retrieved from the Vollard estate, and basking in the adulation of the world. After the interruption of the war, the pace of large exhibitions honoring his work, which had begun in the late thirties, only quickened. He lived to see his vision both understood and honored.

One more word should be said about Rouault as a Catholic artist: Religious art was moribund during the 19th century. Paintings and sculpture were still made on commission for various Christian denominations; yet since no commissions were granted to advanced artists by conservative church bodies, Catholic art little reflected the visual revolution of the last century. All this has changed only since World War II, for many reasons, of course. The simplest is that the Catholic Church itself has reflected the tempo of modern life. It is of course ironic that Rouault, who desired to recapture an older way of life and art-making, should have been taken up as the great modern Catholic artist, and that his timeless, yet peculiarly contemporary vision should be accepted as a valid expression of the religious orientation of our age. He is perhaps existential; his world is that of suffering and melancholy. It is most often genteely French—and rarely if ever escapes into a really savage renunciation of self and world—and yet it speaks with a quiet despair at the human condition.

> "Tomorrow will be beautiful," said the shipwrecked man,
> Before he disappeared beneath the sullen horizon. . . .

wrote the artist as preface to his *Miserere*.

JOSHUA KIND

# GEORGES ROUAULT

**1871**  Born May 27, in a working class suburb of Paris. His father is employed at the Pleyel piano factory.

**1885–90**  Leaves school (1885) to help support his family. Works during the day with the stained-glass restorer Hirsch; at night attends art school.

**1891–95**  Attends the Ecôle des Beaux-Arts after deciding to devote himself to painting. Meets Gustave Moreau, his teacher and life-long inspiration.

**1898–1901**  On Moreau's death (1898), Rouault is appointed curator of the Gustave Moreau Museum. Searches for spiritual stability, and in 1901, spends several months at the Benedictine Abbey at Ligugé, where he meets J. K. Huysmans, the great literary aesthete who has renounced the world and become a Catholic convert.

**1902–05**  With his new "modern style," begins to exhibit, first at the Salon des Indépendants (1902) and later (1903, 1905) at the Salon d'Automne (Autumn Salon), which he helps to found along with Matisse, Huysmans, Redon and others. In 1904, meets the Catholic writer Leon Bloy, who will remain his friend and a major influence.

**1908–11**  Marries Martha Le Sidaner, sister of the artist, Henri. The couple will have four children. In 1910, at the age of 39, has his first one-man show, at the Gallery Druet. In 1911, moves to Versailles, to reduce living costs. Becomes friendly with Raïssa and Jacques Maritain.

**1913–20**  Ambroise Vollard, the influential Parisian art dealer and publisher, buys up all of Rouault's paintings (1913), and in 1917 becomes his exclusive dealer by contract, providing Rouault with the top floor of his home as a studio, thus freeing the artist from material worries.

**1921–30**  During this decade, the artist's fame mounts. The first book on Rouault is published in 1921. In 1924, he is awarded the Legion of Honor. 1930 sees the first Rouault exhibitions outside of France: London, Munich, Chicago, New York. In 1929 he designs sets and costumes for Diaghilev ballet, *The Prodigal Son*.

1938–39   The Museum of Modern Art in New York holds an exhibition of Rouault's prints. Publication of the *Circus of the Shooting Star*. **1939**: Death of Vollard, publication of *The Passion*.

1940–46   Retrospective exhibitions in Boston, Washington, and San Francisco (1940–41). Flees to Southern France when Germans invade; returns to Paris in 1942, where he continues to paint during the war years. Publication of *Divertissement* (1943). Retrospective at Museum of Modern Art, New York (1945). Braque-Rouault Exhibition at Tate Gallery, London (1946).

1947      Rouault's lawsuit against the Vollard family is successful; he recovers more than 700 "unfinished" and unsigned paintings which had been in the art dealer's home at his death in 1939. In the next year, he destroys 315 of these paintings, claiming he is too old to finish them.

1948      Publication of the *Miserere*. Large retrospective in Munich. Visits Italy for the first time.

1951–54   On his 81st birthday (1951), a great public party is held in Paris. Rouault is promoted to Commander of the Legion of Honor. 1952–54: Major exhibitions throughout the world—New York, Tokyo, Los Angeles, Milan, Amsterdam.

1958      Dies in Paris on February 13. He is given a state Funeral.

## Brief Bibliography

Courthion, Pierre, *Georges Rouault,* New York, 1961.

Rouault, Georges, *Miserere* (facsimile edition), intro. by M. Wheeler, New York, 1952.

Venturi, Lionello, *Rouault,* Paris, 1959.

Johnson, Una E., *Ambroise Vollard Editeur,* New York, 1944.

Lansner, K., "Georges Rouault," *Kenyon Review,* vol. 15, no. 3, pp. 455–460.

Wind, E., "Traditional Religion and Modern Art," *Art News,* May, 1953, p. 19 ff.

Fowlie, W., *Jacob's Ladder,* New York, 1947.

Sovy, James T., *Georges Rouault,* New York, 1945.

There is a complete listing of Rouault's own writings on pages 472–473 of Courthion, as well as an extensive bibliography of writings about the artist on the following pages.

15

# NOTES ON THE COLOR PLATES

1. *The Child Jesus Among the Doctors.* 1894. Oil. Musée d'Unterlinden, Colmar. A picture made under the guiding influence of Moreau, whence comes the compositional layout, the small figures in the large architecture, and the dramatic, focused lighting. This work, in its careful drawing of the forms, and very powerful narrative quality, shows a young and sensitive artist already seeking out a source of inspiration—Rembrandt—as intensely involved in the Gospel stories as himself. The Rembrandtesque quality is also evident in the deep shadows, general renunciation of color, and unpretty faces.

2. *The Quarry (The Work Yard).* 1897. Watercolor and pastel. Mr. and Mrs. Henri Simon Collection, Paris. This landscape already presents to us those features which will be common to most of Rouault's paintings of this subject: the small figures in a vast space, and a mood of twilight. Here, in his youth, Rouault has painted an extremely involved narrative where two figures fight in the lower left, and others, armed with scythes, proceed up the rise in the lower right. Put together with the scaffolding and the threatening sky the image might be read as one of almost Symbolist violence and anxiety. But the mood of the work is "literary" and Romantic, and was indebted, as was the earlier religious subject, to the great panorama of Old Master painting at the Louvre with which Rouault was familiar.

3. *The Plain.* 1900. Watercolor. Private Collection, Paris. This work comes from the years of anxiety when Rouault was searching for direction. Under the influence of Moreau, he had disliked the Impressionists for their inconsequential subject matter and their method of working directly from nature. Yet he apparently tried even the latter in the intensity of his effort.

4. *Three Prostitutes.* 1903. Gouache. Hahnloser Collection, Bern. One of his earliest pictures of this subject which he will treat more brutally within a few years (of. Pl. 14).

5. *Tragic Clown.* 1903. Gouache and watercolor. Hahnloser Collection, Bern. Clowns have been a traditional artistic subject in France for centuries. The idea of the clown as a tragic figure originated during the Romantic period, and so well before Rouault there are visual works which show the oppressed figure whose inner being and outer appearance are not in harmony; Daumier, Toulouse-Lautrec, even Watteau in the early 18th century, all used the apparently gay world of the circus as a symbol of life's despair and even madness. It is interesting that in 1903 when Rouault turned to this subject after his spiritual crisis, a young unknown Spanish artist, Picasso, also began a series of clown figures in what is called his "Rose Period." The outward look of the work of both men is quite distinct. Picasso's delicate drawing and coloration, and very specific delineation of posture and facial features are opposed to Rouault's savage color and texture, and his disinterest in the nuances of human expression. Yet although apart in these ways, both Picasso and Rouault are using the image of the clown to convey the pathos of life, and perhaps also the fragility of the artist who alone understands life's horror and attempts to give other men some insight into it.

In this work, Rouault's very free use of watercolor may have to do with his knowledge of the remarkable work by Moreau in a similar expressionist manner. Rouault was familiar with these works in a way few in Paris were at that time, through his assumption of the curator's position at the newly-opened Moreau Museum.

6. *Circus Parade (Clown with Drum).* 1903. Watercolor, gouache and pastel. Private Collection, Paris. Even the extraordinary vivacity of the brushwork cannot conceal the melancholy of this picture.

7. *Versailles (The Fountain).* 1905. Watercolor and pastel. Private Collection, Paris. The dark pessimism of Rouault's outlook is seen even in this view of an ostensibly gay and elegant Versailles. This is one of the few works of Rouault, however, where there is a breath of the real world, where there is no fantasy or interior world feeling, so that the mood of melancholy is not created by a symbol or emblem, but by the transformation of the real. Thus this work is much in contrast to Rouault's later landscapes (cf. Pls. 26, 85), which are really landscapes of the "mind" and related to the Romantic 19th-century

17

"fantastic landscape"—those of Friedrich, for example, and later, of course, Moreau.

8. *The Couple (The Loge)*. 1905. Watercolor and gouache. Private Collection, Switzerland. This painting was one part of a three-part picture entitled *Prostitutes* which Rouault showed in the Autumn Salon of 1905. The works shown in Pls. 9 and 11 may have been the other paintings in the grouping. *The Couple* was inspired by two characters in a novel by Bloy called *The Poor Woman,* and was an attempt by Rouault to portray his revulsion by the middle class. His interpretation did not coincide with that of the book. This is interesting in that even then Rouault did not take himself seriously as a book illustrator; that is, he was moved in a general and not specific way. The Poulots are shown here as "cut-throats," according to Bloy, who despised the picture both for its interpretative inaccuracy and its ugly color and drawing.

9. *Drunken Women*. 1905. Watercolor and pastel. Musée de l'Art Moderne, Paris. Rouault condemns the world's sins in these deep blue works, whose savage, manly drawing bears witness to his passionate concern.

10. *Pitch-Ball Puppets (The Wedding of Nini-Patte-en-l'air)*. 1905. Watercolor. Private Collection, Paris. The proprietress leans gloomily over the counter on which rest the bean bags her customers will throw at the unbreakable dolls. Even in the seemingly innocent street amusement, Rouault finds ongoing gloom and despair, and creates an allegory of human suffering.

11. *Bal Tabarin (Dancing the Chahut)*. 1905. Watercolor and pastel. Musée de l'Art Moderne, Paris. The Chahut was a raucous dance on the order of the Can-Can and had been celebrated by, amongst others, an acid and zany picture by Seurat (now in the Kröller-Müller Museum in Otterlo). Here, in the prevalent blue of that time, the dance becomes oppressive and loses any pleasurable quality.

12. *Head of Christ*. 1905. Watercolor. Collection of Walter P. Chrysler, Jr., New York. Rouault was a careful man and I think carried within him images of the Old Masters garnered at the Louvre and from other sources as well.

The brute force of this work, which in looseness of handling approaches what we in our time call "action" painting, is perhaps even more remarkable if seen as a reinterpretation of a typical large head of Christ of the European tradition —*e.g.*, of da Messina, or Giorgione, or of Rembrandt.

13. *Wrestler (The Parade)*. 1905. Oil and gouache. Musée d l'Art Moderne, Paris. Rouault's sharp caricaturist's eye is seen in this small work where he manipulates oil paint in a loose watercolor technique.

14. *Prostitute*. 1906. Watercolor and pastel. Petit Palais Musée de l'Art, Paris. See Note 15.

15. *Prostitute Before a Mirror*. 1906. Watercolor. Musée de l'Art Moderne, Paris. From his teacher Moreau, Rouault may have inherited the older Romantic period's hatred and fear of women. This literary strain, together with the bourgeois morality that divorced love and sensuality, as well as Bloy's hysterically pitched Catholic eroticism, all move into these pictures of prostitutes. The theme itself was available to Rouault from the late 19th century and the works of Steinlen and Toulouse-Lautrec; Rouault, however, converted these cynical and acrid paintings into ones of loving despair. The predominant blue tone of these pictures, as well as of others of this period, such as Picasso's "Blue Period" works, speaks in a tone of sadness. Add to this (as opposed to Picasso's very delicate, quiet drawing) the violence of Rouault's line, and there comes forth the paradox of his disgust for and love of mankind.

16. *Huckster of a Circus*. 1906. Oil. Private Collection, Tokyo. One of the more colorful pictures of this period, in which the prevalent oppressiveness is abated.

17. *Conjurer*. 1907. Watercolor. Mr. and Mrs. Henri Simon Collection, Paris. A sense of menace and a total lack of any pretense at gaiety characterize this work. Rouault, having learned the technique from his teacher, Moreau, has here smeared the looser watercolor areas with heavy, opaque strokes. Rouault's inner torment is continually expressed in this way: the craft of his art speaks as clearly as the subject itself.

18. *The Condemned Man.* 1907. Oil. Private Collection, Switzerland. See also Pls. 28, 43, 44, 68. The subject of the Judge or the Tribunal has been generally conceived of in terms of the everyday world of legal reality since the late 18th century. Earlier, however, it was the Trial and Judgment of Christ (and beyond that the idea of the Last Judgment) that represented for Western man the ultimate referent in trial scenes. Rouault returned to this older theological or apocalyptic concept—his was a Christian and a Catholic reinterpretation of the subject. *The Condemned Man* is based upon an actual condemnation that he had witnessed in this year, after having arranged visits to courtrooms for himself. He makes his point through the utter simplicity of the arrangement, distinguishing very little between the judges and the judged.

19. *Circus Parade.* 1901. Pastel and gouache. Baugerter Collection, Montreux. It is often forgotten, no doubt because of the external roughness of Rouault's style, that he is extraordinarily precise—in his pre-World War I period—in the description of facial features, postures, even clothing. In one sense this quality survives throughout his work, although in a greatly lessened manner. Compare this work of 1907 with Pl. 41, where, in his so-called "stained-glass" manner of blocks of separated color, the effect is much more schematic.

20. *Nude Raising Her Arms.* 1907. Watercolor and pastel. Musée de l'Art Moderne, Paris. See Note 21.

21. *Bathers.* 1907. Watercolor. Phillip Leclerq Collection The more "neutral" titles of these two works show that they both are traditional nude studies —the interior scene of Pl. 20 perhaps best identified with Degas, the out-of-doors grandeur of Pl. 21 associated with the *Bathers* of Renoir. All the nude paintings in this book show women with their hands raised to their heads—a favorite gesture of the artist and one which is seen also in later work (cf. Pl. 35). At this time, although the posture of the young woman touching her hair (Pl. 20) is like that of the prostitutes of the year before (Pls. 14 and 15), and the color is still somber, the moralizing force is gone. Perhaps one might associate this greater ease and sensuality with Rouault's meeting of his wife-to-be.

22. *The Barge.* 1909. Watercolor and gouache. Museum of Grenoble, France. See Note 23.

23. *Refugees.* 1911. Pastel and gouache. Museum of Art, Zürich. At about this time, a new subject enters the repertory of the artist, the working classes, and one is reminded of the importance for Rouault of Daumier. Work and poverty are never seen as picturesque—only as unremitting despair. The river scene may refer back to the landscapes that he made out-of-doors at the turn of the century, but is now dominated by the expressive blue color.

24. *Slum (Homes of the Wretched).* 1912. Gouache. Hahnloser Collection, Winterthur. See also Pls. 25, 26, 27. After his rejection, at the turn of the century, of the "realistic" landscape tradition of the Impressionists, painted before nature herself, Rouault turns, in works like this, to what may be called an "interior landscape." The scene is very often the suburban working class area where Rouault himself was raised. In this setting he will either inject melancholy actuality (note the two bent-over figures at the lower right of Pl. 25) or he will convert the scene into a dream-vision with the appearance of Christ in the midst of smoke-stacks and red brick (Pl. 26). Rouault will also (as in Pls. 81, 85) paint a long series of "Biblical landscapes" in which the holy figures inhabit an imaginary environment, almost childish in its simplicity.

25. *Landscape.* 1913. Watercolor. Bridgestone Gallery, Tokyo.

26. *Christ in the Suburbs.* 1920. Oil. Fukishima Collection, Tokyo. In his late period, after World War II, Rouault will paint similar pictures. But by then the insistent oppressiveness of the red-brick and smokestack seen here will be transformed into a radiant other-worldliness.

27. *Landscape on a Christmas Day.* 1920. Gouache. Private Collection, Switzerland. One of the rare post-World War I works of Rouault where nature in its actuality is reflected.

28. *Three Judges.* 1924. Oil. Private Collection, Switzerland. Here, in contrast to his earlier paintings, Rouault's wrath is much lessened. This is characteristic of all his work of these years when the great series of prints, the *Miserere*, was in progress and his melancholy was more universal. Nevertheless, he forces

us to see the judges as oppressors by the somberness of the scene—only God may judge man.

29. *Circus Trio.* 1924. Oil. Phillips Collection, Washington. See also Pls. 28–34. Here, and in the following works from the 1920's, the Circus theme becomes for Rouault a means of monumentalizing his despair. In contrast to the caricature and greatly activated brushstrokes of earlier paintings (Pl. 6), these works, in oil paint applied in heavy patches, present the world of the circus as a self-conscious symbol of ironical suffering—the gay show, the meaningless show. Some of the work may be reminiscent of Picasso's Saltimbanques of the c. 1905 period—for instance, the *Old Clown with a Dog* (Pl. 34), or, later, *The Little Family* (Pl. 41), one of the largest of Rouault's paintings; yet the mood of Rouault's grief is always insisted upon in contrast to Picasso's elegant and innocent suffering. Other works (Pls. 30 and 32), in their sharply etched capturing of a glance or expression, do refer back to the earlier work, but are more general in their depiction of the irony of the human condition.

30. *Red-Nosed Clown.* c. 1926. Oil. Private Collection, Tokyo. See Note 29.

31. *Pierrot.* 1925. Oil Bridgestone Gallery, Tokyo. See Note 29.

32. *Profile of a Pierrot.* c. 1925. Oil. Private Collection, Switzerland. Both the severity of the profile view and the downcast glance (both found frequently among Rouault's portrayals of heads) are tangible signs of suffering.

33. *Dancers and a White Dog.* 1925. Oil. Private Collection, Switzerland. See Note 29.

34. *The Old Clown with a Dog.* 1925. Oil. Private Collection, Switzerland. See Note 29.

35. *Nude.* 1925. Oil. Private Collection, U.S.A. In almost the same way as the circus scenes of this time, this very three-dimensional nude, in a posture

like that of the prostitute in Pl. 14, abstractly captures both the vitality and the despair of the flesh. In other words, it is almost a traditional rendition of the nude; the precedent for this in Rouault's works was already set in such paintings as the *Bathers* (Pl. 21).

36. *The Workman's Apprentice (Self-Portrait).* 1925. Oil. Musée d l'Art Moderne, Paris. See also Pl. 38. These two self-portraits (the second of which is said to have been made with the artist's son as model), revert to an old tradition of self-portrayal. Instead of the Romantic insistence upon specific personality, Rouault shows himself in disguise, as artists had done in the earlier Renaissance when self-portraits were rare. The earlier of these works, Pl. 36, was used as the frontispiece of a book on the artist by George Charensol, published in 1926. If not for this occasion, Rouault might not have painted any self-portraits.

37. *Woman Wearing Hat.* c. 1940. Oil. Private Collection, New York. As in many of Rouault's works, the roughened surface, together with the ungracious profile view, create a sense of Medieval and devotional art—an effect so much in contrast to the subject.

38. *Self-Portrait.* 1926. Gouache. Private Collection, U.S.A. See Note 36.

39. *Grotesque.* 1927. Hadorn Collection, Bern. A bizarre, dehumanized humanity is part of the tradition of the caricature, where exaggeration and distortion create an immediate revelation of personality. Rouault, who knew well the French 19th-century caricaturists, headed by Daumier, had toyed with the idea since his earliest mature work, c. 1902, and had already produced some oil masterpieces in this vein (*The Academician, c.* 1913, Art Institute of Chicago, or *Mr. X,* 1911, Albright-Knox Gallery, Buffalo). When he was asked by Vollard to undertake illustrations for his Ubu book, Rouault turned easily to this form of grotesque to convey the essence of avariciousness and stupidity; and this painting was done no doubt to concretize his feelngs about the book illustrations.

40. *Skeleton.* 1932. Gouache. Private Collection. This grizzly painting

may have resulted from Rouault's depiction of several skeletons in the previous years for the *Miserere,* as well as his Catholic feeling for the separation of soul and body—the skeleton representative of all that is mortal. The form of the work is reminiscent of the long predella panel beneath a Medieval altarpiece, where the dead Christ was at times depicted.

41. *Little Family.* 1932. Oil. Private Collection, Paris. There is about this work—one of the largest Rouault ever painted—an almost pathetic sentimentality.

42. *The Time Has Come.* Oil. Illustration for *The Passion.* Private Collection. See Note 71.

43. *Christ Mocked.* c. 1932. Oil. Museum of Modern Art, New York. In these works of the twenties and thirties, the simplified drawing, resulting in the heavy black lines, and the "frozen lava" surfaces of the paint show how really incisive were the paintings of the pre-World War I period. *Christ Mocked,* although easily readable—the leering Semitic faces of the mockers vis-a-vis the patient, downcast face of the Christ—nonetheless has about it an abstract intensity. Although this is not the trial itself, the close confrontation of faces is very much like that in Pl. 68, *The Passion of Christ.*

44. *The Trial of Christ.* 1935. Oil. Fukishima Collection, Tokyo. This savage work shows the Christ seated in what seems a jury box, surrounded, in age-old fashion, by the dull-eyed, uncomprehending and savage world. This work, along with several others in our book, is owned by a Japanese collector. It is of interest that among Rouault's earliest non-European collectors, was Fukishima, who already knew the artist in the 1920's.

45. *Blue Bird.* Watercolor, gouache and oil. Private Collection, Paris. See Note 46.

46. *Equestrienne.* c. 1935. Gouache. Private Collection, Paris. The circus will throughout his life be for Rouault a means of actualizing his feeling of

despair at the pathos of the human condition. Whether seen at arm's length or at a distance, the same kind of eloquent loneliness prevails. One of the artist's insistent motifs to convey this isolation is the downcast glance.

47. *The Dwarf.* 1937. Oil. Art Institute of Chicago. There is about this work a certain quality of the early violence of Rouault's style, but it is transformed by the almost sculptural treatment of the oil paint and the rock-set heaviness of the frontal view of the head. The dwarf as clown is an age-old image of comi-tragedy and Rouault, ever careful of the quality of the glance, here increases the sense of remoteness by the wall-eye.

48. *The Old King.* 1916–37. Oil. Carnegie Institute, Pittsburgh. This, no doubt the most well-known of all Rouault's paintings, is one of the many pictures that he began in Vollard's studio-home, and worked on through many years. It is one of the few Old Testament figures in Rouault's oeuvre, if indeed that is its subject, and its poignancy seems to arise from the sense of mute homage offered by the once powerful, now aged king through the tiny bouquet of flowers. Inspiration for the work may have come from Renaissance portraits in which figures were shown in profile as here, and holding flowers for symbolic reasons—i.e., good luck in marriage. The composition is close to the etched Plate 7 of the *Miserere,* which however is mocking in tone and entitled "We Think Ourselves Kings."

49. *Head of Christ.* 1937–38. Oil. Private Collection, Paris. Usually Rouault's compositions seem quite artless, without contrivance. Here, both the corner placement of the head and its angle set up spatial tensions. In the lower right-hand corner is Rouault's persistent formula for human habitation, the phallus-like, bulbous-headed tower. And it may have been his intention to contrast these two images of death and salvation. Like the previous work, *The Old King,* this painting is close in composition to one of the *Miserere* plates, "Jesus Reviled."

50. *Box Seat.* 1939. Oil. Owned by the artist's family. A rare appearance in Rouault's art of a direct reference to the pomposity and emptiness of the rich.

**51.** *Christ Mocked.* 1939. Oil. Abrams Collection, New York. The typical black-line style of these years, but with a not-at-all encrusted surface, shows the Savior alone. The face, in its shorthand-like notation, is difficult to read in this otherwise fluid painting.

**52.** *Joan of Arc.* 1940–48. Oil. Private Collection, Paris. The sainted leader of the French in their resistance to the English during the 15th century became a resistance symbol as the French organized their underground during the German occupation. The compositional pattern is like that of Rouault's circus horseback riders (cf. Pl. 46) and in the background stands an Ubu-tower, perhaps exemplifying evil. (Also cf. Pl. 87 for a later version of Joan of Arc.)

## *DIVERTISSEMENT*

**53–61, 63–67.** Illustrations for *Divertissement.* 1941–43. Whether or not it was so intended by Rouault, we may today read the title of this collection of Harlequin images as ironic. Published in 1943 by Tériade, in the bitter years of the occupation when the outcome of the struggle was still in doubt, the lithographs created from these charming gouaches must have struck the viewer as, to say the least, odd. The 15 plates, issued in a limited edition of 300, had an accompanying text typical of the poetic prose often composed by Rouault. Aside from the individual poems for each image, there are two introductory poems which may explain the manner in which this enterprise was undertaken by the artist. During wartime depression the artist dreams of his bittersweet youth, which is both conjured up and symbolized by the clown.

The opening poem, "Parade," is an introduction to both the poet and the theme of the work:

> Child of Paris,
> Compassionate village I have never left, . . .
> The beautiful city in black and difficult times—
> Poor dear child, suffering, suffering . . .

And then the following poem bears the same title as the book:

Acrobats and equestrian riders
Tumblers and fantasists
My friends. Color of harmony
Since my most tender infancy
I have been taken with you . . .

We forget for a minute our sad times
When we see you again
Brilliant in the light.

While the atmosphere of these pictures is not joyous, nonetheless they stand quite distant from the profound despair of Rouault's earlier circus scenes, especially those from the first decade of the century. In these works of the war years, there may well be a true reflection of the nostalgia of the opening poems—melancholy, yearning, a desire for the resurrection of both the spirit and youth; and just as the artist's actual youth was overshadowed by poverty and spiritual anxiety, so these images of the clown, the performer and the craftsman aware of the fragility of his art are superficially brilliant but also dark and shadowy. And yet there is no social probing, even though a gamut of human personality is suggested; that past predilection, even obsession, is gone, and the circus of *Divertissement* is a bittersweet circus of the mind, of memory, no longer heightened by the fires of youthful indignation.

The generally accepted lighter quality of this set of circus people is due as well to the lighter color itself, to the material—gouache—which is basically a watercolor, and used here in broad, flat areas which cannot build up to the thick and labored effect of his oils.

53. *Black Pierrot*. 1941. Gouache. (From *Divertissement*.) The sinister quality of the black costume worn by the harlequin is accentuated by the harsh expression on his face. The hands resting folded on the bottom of the picture may show Rouault's acquaintance with this pattern which occurs very often in 15th-century portrait painting, as in the works of Rogier van der Weyden; and may here betoken a fierce inwardness of character, as they effect a severe closure of the picture.

54. *Kindly Bernard*. 1941. Gouache. (From *Divertissement*.) The close-

up focus upon the head and shoulders may here show a greater trust and intimacy —also felt in the large-eyed face. The name Bernard for the French is indelibly linked with the great Medieval monastic-ascetic, St. Bernard of Clairvaux, who inveighed against deliberate artistic extravagance.

55. *Dancers*. 1941. Gouache. (From *Divertissement*.)

56. *Acrobat*. 1941. Gouache. (From *Divertissement*.) The melancholy of the scene, perhaps reminiscent of the torture of the Crucifixion as the acrobat twists before the puppet stage, is reflected in the accompanying poem with its vague phrases about a nameless sorrow.

> Acrobat, with the fine linen helmet,
> If I say today or tomorrow,
> Color and harmony,
> I am far from it. . . .

57. *Wastrel* (*Mangetout*). 1941. Gouache. (From *Divertissement*.) The figure is prepossessing in spite of his overbearing manners recalling Rouault's earlier grotesques and caricatural style.

58. *Madame Yxe*. c. 1940–42. Gouache. (From *Divertissement*.)

59 *Madame Russalka*. 1941. Gouache. (From *Divertiseement*.) The presence of the Russian performer in Rouault's imaginary circus microcosm may have to do with Russian ballet and his feeling for both the artistry and refugee status of the long-time Russian emigrés in Paris.

60. *Grumbler*. 1941. Gouache. (From *Divertissement*.) The long, thin, bearded face is of course very much like Rouault's usual depiction of the face of Christ, yet the side-wise glance and yellow corneas put him apart from the image of suffering.

61. *White Pierrot*. 1941. Gouache. (From *Divertissement*.) The paint-

ing itself is somewhat indecisive, and the poem accompanying the picture speaks of rejection and indifference:

> Poor dear Watteau
> Never has so much been said of you
> But in fact they prefer Boucher
> Certainly easier to be tasted
> In greater numbers. . . .
>
> Perhaps you speak a language
> Rather difficult to understand
> Although they think in agreement
> A mute language. . . .

62. *Pierrot as Aristocrat*. 1941. Oil. Tériade Collection, France. This work, not a part of *Divertissement*, was exhibited along with others in occupied Paris in 1942. In Rouault's catalog statement the artist wrote of the ". . . still distant time when the spirit and the heart of the pilgrim will find really sincere peace. . . ." The sanguine jauntiness of the hands-on-hips posture is also used in *Divertissement* (cf. Plates 57 and 63).

63. *Little Page in Red and Gold*. 1941. Gouache. (From *Divertissement*.)

64. ` *Two Stubborn Men*. 1941. Gouache. (From *Divertissement*.) See also Pl. 66, *The Mocker*. Rouault prefers, for his facial close-ups, either the profile or the frontal view; these are the most direct and "unartful." In this book, it is really only in the two self-portraits (Pls. 36 and 38) that we see the three-quarter view. Somehow these heads remind us of the ever-presence of the Passion for Rouault, and suggest the tormentors of Christ, as in Pl. 68, and also recall Plate 40 of the *Miserere*, entitled "Face to Face."

65. *Margo*. 1941. Gouache. (From *Divertissement*.) Again with down-cast eyes, the figure suggests a humbled sadness.

66. *The Mocker*. 1941. Gouache. (From *Divertissement*.) See Note 64.

67. *Harlequin.* 1943. Gouache. (From *Divertissement.*) The concluding image of Rouault's wartime world, dressed in black and gold, like a "lubricious wasp," stands with a semi-decisive gesture beckoning to us as the curtain falls.

> In this last harlequinade
> Fifteenth of the cycle . . .
> I love to see you a last time
> To evoke in fantasy
> Yellow of gold and black of ivory . . .
> The one lubricious wasp
> Watching over living and dead
> In these sad times
> For a dance of death.

Suddenly, the gentle-seeming clown has become a harbinger of death.

68. *The Passion of Christ.* 1943. Oil. Collection of Mr. and Mrs. Leigh B. Block, Chicago. This work raises the problem of renunciation in an artist. The intricate arrangement of the figures and deft distinctions of physiognomies easily single out this painting among the predominant number of works with simple images, which he most often preferred. Also, there is in the lower left hand figure a rare appearance in Rouault's work of a profile moving toward a three-quarter view. Thus the scene, with its juxtaposed facial views, cut off by the frame in various ways, becomes strangely nervous despite the apparent symmetry. Rouault was clearly capable of such complexities, but usually denied them.

69. *The Flight into Egypt.* 1945. Oil. Private Collection, Paris. See Note 70.

70. *Christ in the House of Martha and Mary.* c. 1945. Oil. Private Collection, Paris. Rightly enough, these glowing, jewel-like paintings have been compared to Medieval Christian art with its equivalent transcendental force. Yet such comparisons are partially aimed at inducing an easier acceptance of them by the recalcitrant; actually, the vagueness of the drawing, the strong colors and the rich textures all mark these works and others like them as un-

mistakably of our time. And perhaps it would not be out of place to label them "Gallic" as well, for just these reasons.

## *THE PASSION*

71. *The Raising of Lazarus.* Oil. Illustration for *The Passion.* See also Pls. 42, 75–78. These six paintings are part of a series done by Rouault between 1930–1938 as illustrations, or more accurately "interpretations," of the text *The Passion* by André Suarès (1868–1948). Suarès was a Catholic writer who had been Rouault's friend since 1911—their reticent temperaments were well suited to each other. In fact, Rouault could write to Suarès: "You are, after Gustave Moreau, the one spirit by whom I feel I have the most complete understanding, even though you are not a painter." Suarès' text may be called a series of poetic meditations on the scenes of Christ's Passion, and Rouault's pictures—54 paintings in all, which became the source of the book's black and white woodcuts—are like glowing, yet obscure dream-images accompanying the drama.

Pls. 42 and 76 are illustrations from the chapter entitled "Veronica." Suarès uses the legend (described in the note to Pl. 72) obscurely and instead presents a conversation between two unidentified people, obviously intended as Christ and Veronica. The sensuous text speaks with the long tradition of Catholic mystic symbolism and is also reminiscent of the text of Bach's Cantata No. 140:

Veronica: You are the single presence and I hide myself. Is it because of the excess of my joy or the shame and agony of my indignity? Love, you are the delight of my sadness.

Christ: Your looks are full of me and you do not recognize O woman, woman, that says everything and nothing.

Veronica: I see it well, my beloved, between the world and you I am a veil for a divine instant . . . veil of love, mirror without a blemish . . .

Rouault's pictures bear only occasional reference to the words, so that Pl. 42 shows Christ confronted by his executioners, and Pl. 76 shows the Veil of Veronica upheld behind Christ as he carries his Cross on his shoulders.

Pl. 71 is the illustration for the chapter entitled "Before the House of Lazarus," and shows Christ beckoning to Lazarus as he rises at the lower right. (It should be remarked that Rouault's oil paintings were converted by the mastercraftsman Georges Aubert into woodcuts for printing, and in this process —overseen by Rouault throughout its entire length—the relative unclarity of the reproduced oils was eliminated. Therefore, in the actual book itself, it is easier to read the image.) The most telling lines of the chapter are those spoken by Jesus:

> Lazarus is my friend. Lazarus is not dead.
> He is more dead in his person of evil life
> Than he who is asleep in the bosom of the earth.

Pl. 75, a lamentation over the body of Christ taken from the Cross, is the image for the chapter, "The Man Who Brought Myrrh" (L'Homme à la Myrrh). Here the text invokes the victory of Christ over mortal degradation:

> Here he is brought down to our level. He whom
> They raised nearer to the heavens to laugh at.
> The jeers make a white pedestal which is higher
> Than the clouds.

Pl. 77, *The Crucifixion* is the last illustration for the chapter entitled "Disciples," where an hallucinatory city landscape—very much like a typical Rouault city scene—is described:

> A road of red lava flows from the sun in
> The center of the deserted place.
> And far away, at the edge of the fairy-like
> Carpet stretched out on the leprosy of the
> Surroundings, a tower is raised more terrible
> Than the turban of stone where the Parsis offer
> The vultures the naked flesh of the dead.

It has been said that no Christ depicted by Rouault ever shows the Stigmata, the wounds of the Cross. If this is so—and note that Pl. 77 cuts off the image at the wrists and knees—then this perhaps unconscious gesture by the artist might be an attempt to underplay the suffering and present the Savior as more than a human figure. This is somewhat strange in the light of Rouault's friendship with Bloy who was so dominated by the gospel of human suffering and wrote: "In his poor heart man has places which do not yet exist, and suffering enters in order to bring them to life." Rouault's painting shows Christ surrounded by angels at the sides, in a rigid, other-worldly format that recalls late Medieval art patterns.

Pl. 78 is the well-known subject *Ecce Homo*, Behold This Man, in which Christ is presented to the crowd for judgment. In our set of reproductions it is closest to being a literal illustration, and was made for the chapter entitled "Ecce Dolor." The composition of the work may have been influenced by Rouault's knowledge of early 16th-century German graphic art, for instance, Dürer's Passion series. The image however is far gentler than the text:

> Look at this forehead and Christ's skin of blood.
> His hair is plaited with the purple ribbons of flesh.
> His cheeks are furrowed with red ravines.

72. *Veronica.* c. 1945. Oil. Private Collection, Paris. Rouault's intensely sentimental Catholicism obviously led him to this most warmly human of the miracles of the Passion story. The story of Veronica comes from the Apocryphal gospel of Nicodemus, where it is told that Christ's sufferings on his way to Calvary so moved this young woman that she wiped his sweat with her veil. Afterwards her veil bore the image of the Savior's visage upon it. Here, in a portrait of the Saint herself, Rouault gives her the aspect of a nun by placing her veil upon her head.

73. *Holy Face.* c. 1946. Oil. Private Collection, Paris. See Note 74.

74. *Holy Face.* c. 1940's. Oil. Private Collection. See also Pl. 73. Although our examples here are from the 1940's, Roualt had painted this subject much in the same way as early as 1912. The mystery and miracle of his faith is summed up in this supremely visual and concrete image, which must have deeply moved him both as a Catholic and as an artist. He also must have enjoyed this particular subject since nothing more was called for than a flat and frontal representation, Medieval in a sense, which coincided with his usual penchant for simple, uncomplicated compositions.

75. *Lamentation.* Oil. Illustration for *The Passion.* See Note 71.

76. *The Veil of Veronica Upheld.* Oil. Illustration for *The Passion.* See Note 71.

77. *The Crucifixion.* Oil. Illustration for *The Passion.* See Note 71.

78. *Ecce Homo.* Oil. Illustration for *The Passion.* See Note 71.

83. *Homo Homini Lupus.* 1940–44. Oil. Musée de l'Art Moderne, Paris. The title of the work, *Man is a Wolf to Man* (a phrase from the *Asinaria* of Plautus) had been used by Rouault for Plate 37 of the *Miserere,* where a martial skeleton is shown. Here, while a village burns, and beneath a red sun, the eternal drama of man's inhumanity to man is depicted by an artist who has been obsessed with suffering, but rarely because of man-made war.

## THE LATE WORKS

### (*Plates 79–82, 84–92*)

In the years following World War II, Rouault, now over 70, entered into the style of his old age. Although some of his works of this period may have been among those recovered from the Vollard family in the famous lawsuit of 1947, they were nevertheless "finished" by the artist in the shorthand of old age, perhaps analogously to the last works of Rembrandt or Michelangelo. Rouault had of course throughout his life emphasized the power of the non-descriptive element of the visual art; and now his work becomes increasingly hazy, encrusted, glowing.

While his subject matter did not change—the New Testament scenes, clowns, and "interior" landscapes still recur—the mood of these works is somehow diffuse. Seemingly in work as recent as the gouaches for *Divertissement* in the early 1940's, he still wished to paint crisply with a certain kind of intensity. Now, however, as in *Biblical Landscape* (Pl. 84), or *Onesimus* (Pl. 86), whether the focus is near or far, small or large, the entire work is seen with a more blurred vision, and the mood is more other-worldy. It is during this time that he made a long series of autumnal landscapes as in Pl. 81, where the mood is a joyous melancholy, the resignation and knowingness of old age. Life's fulfillment is at hand and there is a continual sense of resolution as figures whom we sense are Christ and the apostles wander through scenes which at times (as in Pl. 85) dissolve entirely in the blur of memory. Compare, for instance, the two Saint Joans, the one from 1939 (Pl. 52), with its clear delineation of Joan's upheld neck, and the 1951 work (Pl. 87), with its vaporous dissolution of form in a thick crust of paint. In these late works, I am reminded of the work of Albert Ryder, the late-19th-century American Romantic artist who also worked in a richly encrusted world of melancholy; but more to the point would be the resemblance of such of Rouault's work to the little-known color abstractions of Moreau, an influence which dates back before 1900.

A note about the "Ubu-tower" which has been a recurrent feature of Rouault's landscapes for decades, and which occurs also in these late works. The name comes from the *Palace of King Ubu*, an illustration which Rouault had made for a book by Vollard called *The Reincarnation of Father Ubu*. Ubu was a fantastic and dissolute character, the sum of man's viciousness and evil, who had been invented by Alfred Jarry in his play *Ubu Roi* (1894). For Rouault, however, this tower cannot have meant evil alone since it occurs peacefully in many of these "Biblical Landscapes" (cf. Pl. 85).

79. *The Cumaean Sibyl.* 1947. Private Collection, New York. Both lines and color areas here and in Pl. 80 are still surprisingly firm, and it may be that these two works are among the pre-World War II paintings returned by the Vollard family.

80. *Two Clowns.* c. 1947. Private Collection, New York.

81. *Autumn.* 1948. Oil. The Vatican Museum, Rome.

82. *De Profundis.* 1948. Oil. Private Collection, Japan.

84. *Biblical Landscape.* 1949. Oil. Private Collection, Paris. In works like this from the last years of his life, it is as if the artist is totally disinterested in any effect other than a disembodied tranquility.

85. *Biblical Landscape.* 1949. Oil. Private Collection, Paris. By cutting off the figures with the frame, Rouault has made here a more "sophisticated" effect than is usual in these late works. The Ubu tower, here clearly connoting no evil, stands in the distance.

86. *Onesimus.* 1952. Oil. Private Collection, Paris. Behind this clown's Latinate name, there lies perhaps a word play, "we are burdened." Also unusual is the placement of the head next to the margin of the image; Rouault's heads are most often centered.

87. *Saint Joan.* 1951. Oil. Private Collection, Paris. (Cf. Pl. 52.)

88. *Moonlight.* 1952. Oil. Private Collection, Paris. The late landscapes are like a litany, reiterating a similar statement to the point of hypnosis.

89. *Decorative Flowers.* c. 1953. Oil. Private Collection, Paris. Rouault, who had rarely made traditional still-lifes (that is, simply collections of inanimate objects such as flowers or food), produced a good number of floral images in the last two decades of his life. The one reproduced here is typical, with its abundant collection of imaginary blooms surrounded by a painted frame—a device also seen in the late works of Braque.

90. *Jerusalem.* 1954. Oil. Private Collection, Tokyo. Like glowing bits of jewelry, these last works are set within their own frames and exist in a remote, mysterious realm. His melancholy is always tempered by a kind of joy—his ongoing approach through his Catholicism to the suffering inherent in life.

91. *Sarah.* 1956. Oil. Private Collection, Paris.

92. *Theodora.* 1956. Oil. Private Collection, Paris.

# THE PLATES

1 *The Child Jesus Among the Doctors.* 1894. Oil. 29½ × 22 in. Musée d'Unterlinden, Colmar. Even at the outset, Rouault eschewed sweetness in telling the story of Christ.

2  *The Quarry (The Work Yard)*.  1897.  Watercolor and pastel.  24¾ × 33½ in.  Mr. and Mrs. H. Simon Coll., Paris.  The confusion of mood reflects dissatisfaction with Romantic painting.

3  *The Plain.*   1900.   Watercolor.   6¾ × 7⅛ in.   Private Collection, Paris.   Rarely after this time would Rouault's work portray the world of nature.

4 *Three Prostitutes.* 1903. Gouache. Hahnloser Collection, Bern. Rouault's disordered-seeming yet deft brush strokes underscore the meaning of this subject.

5  *Tragic Clown*.  1903.  Gouache and watercolor.  4¼ × 5⅜ in.  Hahnloser Collection, Bern. The age-old image of superficial gaiety and internal suffering.

6  *Circus Parade (Clown with Drum).*    1903.    Watercolor, gouache and pastel.    12½ × 9½ in.
Private Collection, Paris.    Note the virtuosity with which the facial features are defined.

7 *Versailles* (*The Fountain*). 1905. Watercolor and pastel. 24¾ × 21 in. Priv. Coll., Paris.
Angular strokes, unclear drawing, and dank color deliberately destroy the splendor of this scene.

8  *The Couple (The Loge).*  1905.  Watercolor and gouache.  25⅜ × 17⅞ in.  Priv. Coll.,
Switz.   Life's degradation is his insistent subject matter—here inspired by the novelist Bloy.

9 *Drunken Woman*. 1905. Watercolor and pastel. 27½ × 21¼ in. Musée de l'Art Moderne, Paris. The undeniable ugliness of this subject aroused the sincere anger of many critics.

10 *Pitch-Ball Puppets* (*The Wedding of Nini-Patte-en-l'air*). 1905. Watercolor. 20½ × 26⅜ in. Private Collection, Paris. For Rouault, even amusements become allegories of life's suffering.

11 *Bal Tabarin* (*Dancing the Chahut*). 1905. Watercolor and pastel. 27½ × 21¼ in. → Musée de l'Art Moderne, Paris. Sexuality and joy, seen through a veil of despair, become degraded and sour.

12  *Head of Christ*.  1905.  Oil on paper.  44¾ × 31 in.  Coll. W. P. Chrysler. Jr., N.Y.  Here, Rouault indicates his own torment at the Passion with paint almost thrown on the surface.

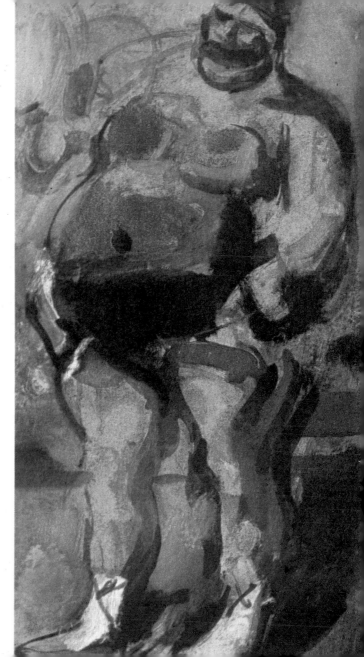

13
*Wrestler* (*The Parade*). 1905.
Oil and gouache. 8¾ × 5⅞ in.
Musée de l'Art Moderne, Paris.
Rouault's on-going theme: the
irony of the human condition and
the ever-presence of suffering.

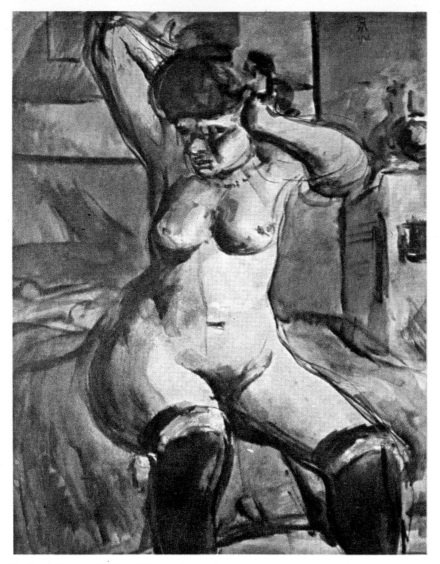

14 *Prostitute*.   1906.   Watercolor and pastel.   28 × 21⅝ in.   Petit Palais Musée de l'Art, Paris.   The artist's poverty often forced him to use women of the streets as models.

15 *Prostitute Before a Mirror*.  1906.  Watercolor.  28⅜ × 21⅝ in  Musée de l'Art Moderne, Paris.  Rouault's precise technique is illustrated by the similarities between this and Pl. 14.

16 *Huckster of a Circus* **1906.** Oil. 10⅝ × 17½ in. Private Collection, Tokyo. The fun circus of Degas and Renoir is denied here by the heavy contours and somber color.

17 *Conjurer*.  1907.  Watercolor.  17½ × 13 in.  Mr. and Mrs. Henri Simon Coll., Paris.  A forerunner of the artist's later caricatures, this work is marked by a rare malevolence.

18 *The Condemned Man*. 1907. Oil. 28⅞ × 41 in. Priv. Coll., Switzerland. In these years, Rouault's art fed upon life; and he actually attended court sessions to absorb the atmosphere.

19 *Circus Parade*.  1907.  Pastel and gouache.  25⅝ × 41¼ in.  Baugerter Collection, Montreux.  Note how amid the loose array of lines, suddenly the facial features are sharply in focus.

20 *Nude Raising her Arms.* 1907. Watercolor and pastel. 12⅛ × 12 in. Musée de l'Art Moderne, Paris. Here, the moral condemnation seems diminished, and a sensual power is asserted.

21 *Bathèrs*.   1907.   Watercolor.   38½ × 25½ in.   Phillip Leclerq Collection.   This unusual work is one of the most decorative and traditional of Rouault's female nudes.

22 *The Barge.* 1909. Watercolor and gouache. 22¾ × 34⅝ in. Museum of Grenoble, France. The life of the poor, which Rouault knew well, was a new theme in his art.

3 *Refugees*.  1911.  Pastel and gouache.  17¾ × 23⅝ in.  Mus. of Art, Zürich.  With a repetition reminiscent of litany, and perhaps with a similar aim, the artist presents man's oppression.

24
*Slum* (*Homes of the Wretched*). 1912. Gouache. Hahnloser Collection, Winterthur, Switzerland. A somber and despressing image—both the houses and the faceless people have no significance.

25 *Landscape*. 1913. Watercolor. 8⅛ × 12¼ in. Bridgestone Gallery, Tokyo. The pale watercolor wash and abbreviated drawing accentuate the hopeless emptiness.

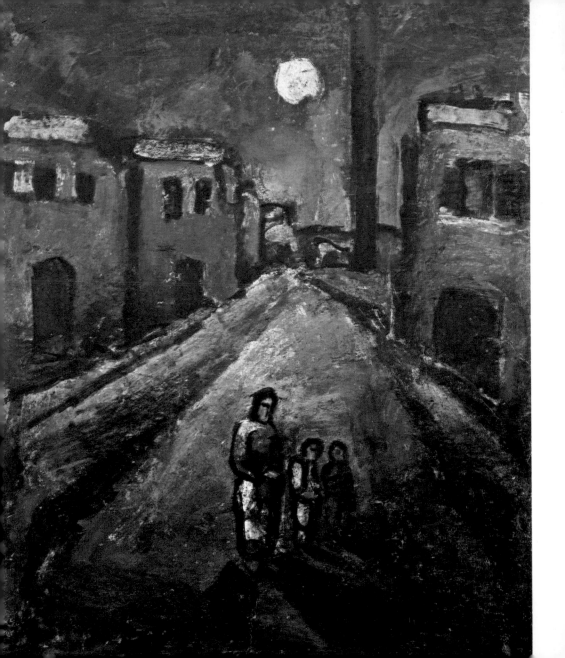

←26 *Christ in the Suburbs.* 1920. Oil. 36¼ × 29⅛ in. Fukishima Collection, Tokyo. In the middle of the empty street, surrounded by gaping-mouthed brick houses, the Hope of the World offers solace to children.

27 *Landscape on a Christmas Day.* 1920. Gouache. 18⅞ × 26¼ in. Private Collection, Switzerland. The force of this picture lies in the irony created by the use of a pacific title for this bleak and inhospitable scene.

28  *Three Judges.*  1924  Oil.  29⅞ × 41½ in.  Private Collection, Switzerland.  Rich color
and high seriousness produce a scene sympathetic to the judge's ordeal in his search for truth.

29 *Circus Trio*. 1924. Oil. 29⅞ × 41⅞ in. Phillips Collection, Washington. Both the downcast eyes and block-like bodies evoke that mood of suffering so frequent in Rouault's work.

30  *Red-Nosed Clown.*  c. 1926.  Oil.  29½ × 20½ in.  Private Collection, Tokyo.  Rouault's circus people are especially poignant carriers of suffering since their costumes mock their tragedy.

31  *Pierrot.*  1925.  Oil.  29¾ × 20⅛ in.  Bridgestone Gallery, Tokyo.  Somber heads such as this one recall Cézanne's early fierce works (c. 1865–70).

32  *Profile of a Pierrot*.  c. 1925.  Oil.  25⅛ × 18⅛ in.  Priv. Coll., Switzerland.  Rouault portrays a mood of resigned sadness that often becomes more important than the subject.

33 *Dancers and a White Dog.* 1925. Oil. 26¾ × 19⅝ in. Priv. Coll., Switzerland. At the time, the artist was not interested in detail; faces and hands are deliberately blurred.

34  *The Old Clown with a Dog.*  1925.  Oil.  28¾ × 18⅞ in.  Priv. Coll., Switzerland.  These private scenes of circus performers remind one of the fragile delicacy of Picasso's Blue Period.

35 *Nude*. 1925. Oil. 31½ × 23⅝ in. Private Collection, U.S.A. A powerful work where the robustness of paint and contour vie with the tiredness of the figure for dominance of mood.

36 *The Workman's Apprentice (Self-Portrait)*. 1925. Oil. 26 × 20½ in. Musée de l'Art Moderne, Paris. Rouault's art is subjective, yet this is one of very few self-portraits.

**37** *Woman Wearing Hat.* c. 1940. Oil. 13 × 9½ in. Private Collection, New York. The elongated neck—representing both strain and spirit—is fairly frequent in Rouault's work.

38 *Self-Portrait*. 1926. Gouache. 22¼ × 16 in. Private Collection, U.S.A. In his rare self-portraits, Rouault shows himself as a humble worker (Pl. 36) or tragi-comic clown.

39 *Grotesque*.   1927.   12¼ × 9 in.   Hadorn Collection, Bern.   Rouault's clowns are "wise fools" who laugh as their hearts break; this empty fool is to be pitied for his lack of feeling.

40 *Skeleton*.  1932.  Gouache.  3⅛ × 8⅝ in.  Private Collection.  Symbol of all that is mortal
· and the end of earthly suffering, the grim skeleton presents no threat to the believer.

**41**
*Little Family.*
1932. Oil. 81⅞ ×
45⅜ in. Private
Collection, Paris.
Many are moved by
Rouault's humble-
ness, many are re-
pelled by his morbid
awkwardness; an
admirer made a rug
of this image.

42 *The Passion: The Time Has Come.* Oil. Private Collection. At times the crust of paint in Rouault's work creates a dream-like effect, which here belies the violence of the event.

43 *Christ Mocked.* c. 1932. Oil. 35¾ × 28½ in. Museum of Modern Art, New York. The crackle of paint, black outlines, and lack of traditional symbols, move this work into our age.

44
*The Trial of Christ.* 1935.
Oil. 30 × 41⅜ in. Fukishima
Collection, Tokyo. In contrast
to the sharply etched quality of
the previous work, this one has a
primitive crudity.

**45** *Blue Bird*.   Watercolor, gouache and oil.   22¾ × 16½ in.   Priv. Coll., Paris.   The gentle delicacy only slightly relieves the prevailing sadness of the downcast eyes and somber color.

46 *Equestrienne*. c. 1935. Gouache. 18½ × 15⅜ in. Private Collection. Paris. At times, Rouault painted frames around his works—as if in an effort to isolate them.

47 *The Dwarf.* 1937. Oil. 27⅛ × 19¾ in. Art Institute of Chicago. Gap-toothed and wall-eyed, this thick faced clown seems to suggest the paradox which unites suffering and evil.

48 *The Old King*.   **1916–37.**   Oil.   **30¼ × 21½** in.   Carnegie Institute, Pittsburgh.   In a sense, this work sums up Rouault's message: Man should recognize the limits of his power.

49 *Head of Christ*. 1937–38. Oil. 26⅜ × 18⅞ in. Private Collection, Paris. The jewel-like color and swift elegance of the brush stroke contrast oddly with the introspection of Christ.

50  *Box Seat*.  1939.  Oil.  31⅞ × 25⅛ in.  Owned by the artist's family.  Both the blue color and the undefined faces create a vapidity emblematic of the false values of this world.

51 *Christ Mocked*. 1939. Oil. 23⅝ × 16½ in. Abrams Coll., New York. Our impression of this work is so precise, it is difficult to believe that the face and hands are so vague.

52  *Joan of Arc.*  1940–48.  Oil.  26¼ × 18⅞ in.  Priv. Coll., Paris.  This saint's dream-like life of visionary ecstasy and martyrdom held great fascination for Rouault's friend Leon Bloy.

53 *Black Pierrot*. 1941. Gouache. 13 × 8½ in. Tériade Collection, France. These charming works, lacking the crustiness of oil paint, were created during the oppressive war years.

54 *Kindly Bernard*. 1941. Gouache. 12½ × 9½ in. Tériade Collection, France. For Rouault, a wide-eyed direct glance is an attribute of innocence.

**55** *Dancers.* **1941.** Gouache. 11 × 8⅞ in. Tériade Coll., France. It is odd, considering the precision of Rouault's facial close-ups, that he made the episodic scenes so blurred.

56 *Acrobat*. 1941. Gouache. 10⅝ × 8⅞ in. Tériade Collection, France. This is somehow the bleakest of the set, suggesting a torment of the flesh.

57 *Wastrel* (*Mangetout*). 1941. Gouache. 12⅝ × 9½ in. Tériade Collection, France. This figure suggests the tradition of caricature by the small body and large head.

58 *Madame Yxe*.　c. 1940–42.　11 × 8⅝ in.　Tériade Coll., France.　Rouault rarely represents lips with only a thin, brief line as here; this painting implies tense anxiety and introspection.

59 *Madame Russalka*.   1941.   Gouache.   Tériade Collection, France.   The dancer here seems to have a more buoyant personality than her companion in Pl. 58.

60  *Grumbler*.  1941.  Gouache.  Tériade Collection, France.  Even the unflattering appellation given this member of the troupe does not affect Rouault's sympathy.

61 *White Pierrot*. 1941. Gouache. 10¾ × 8½ in. Tériade Collection, France. Compared
with his black counterpart (Pl. 53), white Pierrot is vague and insubstantial.

62 *Pierrot as Aristocrat.* 1941. Oil. 44¼ × 27⅞ in. Tériade Coll., France. Surely one of Rouault's most optimistic works, which in its brilliant color anticipates his late landscapes.

63 *Little Page in Red and Gold*.   1941.   Gouache.   12¼ × 9⅞ in.   Tériade Coll., France.
Round faces are infrequent in the work of Rouault; they betoken a good humor, as here.

64
*Two Stub-
born Men*.
1941.
Gouache.
Tériade
Collection,
France.
These men
look
strangely
familiar:
Could
they be
Christ's
tormen-
tors? (See
Pl. 43.)

**65** *Margo.* 1941. Gouache. 12 × 9½ in. Tériade Collection, France. The color and cheeky plumpness of this figure, and the exuberance of her name, give this work a jaunty quality.

66 *The Mocker*. 1941. Gouache. 11¾ × 10 in. Tériade Collection, France. For Rouault, the sharp-nosed figure (as in Pls. 30 and 43) is malicious and causes suffering.

67  *Harlequin.*  1943.  Gouache.  11¼ × 9 in.  Tériade Collection, France.  The drama of *Divertissement* (the previous 15 plates) ends with a wistful wave as the curtain falls.

68  *The Passion of Christ.*  1943.  Oil.  41 × 29 in.  Collection of Mr. and Mrs. Leigh B. Block, Chicago.  One of the most subtle of Rouault's compositions, enhanced by the dispersed glances of the solemn figures.

69 *The Flight into Egypt*. 1945. Oil. 24 × 18½ in. Priv. Coll., Paris. In its hidden suggestiveness, this work refers back to the Symbolist mode of the artist's early period.

**70** *Christ in the House of Martha and Mary.* c. 1945. Oil. 18⅛ × 25⅝ in. Private Collection, Paris. Both the glowing colors and the over-all vagueness strongly suggest a dream image.

71 *The Passion: The Raising of Lazarus.* 1930–38. Oil. 'Private Collection. In these almost magical biblical illustrations, the omnipresent mood of oppressiveness is markedly lifted.

72 *Veronica.* c. 1945. Oil. 19¾ × 14¼ in. Private Collection, Paris. As in Christ's face on her veil (cf. Pl. 73), Veronica's innocence is felt in her wide-eyed glance.

73 *Holy Face.* c. 1946. Oil. 19⅝ × 11 in. Priv. Coll., Paris. This portrayal of Christ's visage may be the standard depiction of our time—much as Rembrandt's were in years past.

74 *Holy Face.* c. 1940's. Oil. Private Collection. The veil, now with an image of downcast→ sorrow, is shown here in an Hebraic tabernacle.

**76** *The Passion: The Veil of Veronica Upheld.* 1930–38. Oil. Priv. Coll. As in Pl. **77** the symmetry and obscure spatiality create the sense of an emblem rather than a scene.

77  *The Passion: Crucifixion.*  1930–38.  Oil.  Private Collection.  Christ is felt to be both human and inhuman here, as the image fluctuates between immediacy and abstraction.

78 *The Passion: Ecce Homo.* 1930–38. Oil. Private Collection. "Behold this man," cries Pilate, and the scene blurs as if it were some dimly recalled moment.

**79** *The Cumaean Sibyl.* 1947. 20½ × 14½ in. Priv. Coll., N.Y. The pagan prophetess, best known through Michelangelo's Sistine Chapel painting, is shown with an oracular gesture.

80  *Two Clowns*.   c. 1947.   Private Collection, New York.   An interesting pairing of antithetical personalities: the guileful and the naive.

81
*Autumn*. 1948. Oil. 26¾ × 41¼ in.
The Vatican Museum, Rome. These
rich and exotic, yet melancholy late landscapes are indicative of the on-going
influence which Moreau exerted on
Rouault.

82 *De Profundis*.  1948.  Oil.  11¾ × 8¼ in.  Priv. Coll., Japan.  "From the depths"—the ancient cry of the distressed soul—is translated into a setting of hope and salvation.

83 *Man is a Wolf to Man,* 1940–44. Oil. 25⅝ × 18⅛ in. Musée de l'Art Moderne, Paris. Nowhere is Rouault's condemnation of mankind more stark than here.

**84** *Biblical Landscape.* 1949. Oil. 13 × 17¾ in. Private Collection, Paris. Christ and the apostles wander in peace and tranquility as the aged artist projects dream images.

85  *Biblical Landscape*.   1949.   Oil.   13 × 17¾ in.   Priv. Coll., Paris.   In a darker terrain, the holy figures seem protected by a tree which bends as they do.

86  *Onesimus*.  1952.  Oil.  15⅛ × 9¼ in.  Priv. Coll., Paris.  In deep old age, like other masters who had reached past the biblical limit, Rouault works in an abbreviated manner.

87 *Saint Joan*. 1951. Oil. 11¾ × 9½ in. Private Collection, Paris. A few brief strokes serve here to indicate the vision of the heroic sainted figure.

88 *Moonlight*. 1952. Oil. 18⅛ × 13 in. Private Collection, Paris. These late blurred visions are filled with a glowing serenity; the artist's torment approaches resolution.

89 *Decorative Flowers.* c. 1953. Oil. 37 × 25¼ in. Priv. Coll., Paris. Still-lifes are infrequent in Rouault's career—perhaps because of his conviction about the religious role of art.

90 *Jerusalem*. 1954. Oil. 27⅛ × 21¼ in. Priv. Coll., Tokyo. Hazy and warm, charming and almost naïve, the painting presents, in Rouault's old-age style, a world removed from care.

91 *Sarah*. 1956. Oil. 21⅝ × 16½ in. Private Collection, Paris. Throughout his career, such oval faces have signified inner freedom and wisdom to the artist.

92 *Theodora*. 1956. Oil. 25½ × 17¾ in. Private Collection, Paris. Rouault's last period returns to his earliest Romanticism and its exotic splendor.